30 Days of Praise

Praising My Way to My Breakthrough

Debbie Snooks-Aiken

Praising My Way to My Breakthrough

SJ Writing Services LLC
Publishing
Columbia, South Carolina
sjwritingservices.com

Copyright © 2025 by Debbie Snooks-Aiken

First Edition: 2025

All rights reserved. No part of this publication may be reproduced, distributed, transmitted in any form or by any means, stored in a database or retrieval system, electronic, mechanical, photocopying, recording, scanning, or otherwise, without written permission from the publisher. It is illegal to copy this book, post it on a website, or distribute it by any other means without written permission from the copyright owner, Debbie Snooks-Aiken.

Scriptures from the New Living Translation (NLT)
Book Cover Design
SJ Writing Services LLC

ISBN: 978-1-967699-04-9

Praising My Way to My Breakthrough

Table of Contents

Dedication..................................1

Day 1......................................2

Day 2......................................5

Day 3......................................8

Day 4......................................11

Day 5......................................14

Day 6......................................17

Day 7......................................20

Day 8......................................23

Day 9......................................26

Day 10....................................29

Day 11....................................32

Day 12....................................35

Day 13....................................38

Day 14....................................41

Day 15....................................44

Day 16....................................47

Day 17....................................50

Day 18....................................53

Day 19....................................56

Day 20....................................59

Day 21....................................63

Day 22....................................66

Day 23.................................70
Day 24.................................73
Day 25.................................76
Day 26.................................79
Day 27.................................83
Day 28.................................87
Day 29.................................90
Day 30.................................94
About the Author........................97

Dedication

This book is lovingly dedicated to my husband, Gerard Aiken, whose unwavering love and faith have been a steady light through every season of my life. Thank you for walking beside me, covering me in prayer, and believing in the vision God placed within me.

To my precious children — Gerald, Kenya, Kenyon, and Kaleb — you are my heart's greatest blessings and the purest reflection of God's grace. Your laughter has been my strength, your love my anchor, and your presence my daily reminder of why faith and perseverance matter.

May this work stand as a testament to the power of God's love, the beauty of family, and the strength that lives within us when we trust His divine plan.

Praising My Way to My Breakthrough

Day 1

"Let everything that breathes sing praises to the Lord! Praise the Lord!"

Psalm 150:6

Praising My Way to My Breakthrough

Ssshhhh! Listen to that. Do you hear that? That is your Every breath we take is a gift from God — a reminder of His grace that sustains us. The psalmist calls all creation to join in one great symphony of praise. The birds sing, the wind whispers, the oceans roar, and even the stars declare His glory.

We, too, are instruments of His praise. When we lift our voices, when we serve in love, when we choose peace over chaos — we are praising the Lord with our lives. Praise is not just a sound; it's a posture of the heart. It turns our focus from what we lack to the One who provides.

Let everything within you — your joy, your tears, your victories, and your struggles — become praise unto the Lord. For He is worthy, and His mercy endures forever.

Most Glorious and precious Savior. I thank you for your loving kindness. I thank you for life, health, and strength. I know that I sometimes take life for granted, but you have never turned against me. I am forever grateful that you breathe your breath of life into me so I may be in your presence once more. Tomorrow is not a promise, so I asked you, Father, to order my steps and direct my path. Please help me to focus on today and trust that you have it all in control. Let your will be done in my life today and forever more.

In your Son, Jesus' name, Amen.

Scripture Reflection

Day 2

"O Lord, I will honor and praise your name, for you are my God. You do such wonderful things! You planned them long ago, and now you have accomplished them."

Isaiah 25:1

Isaiah's declaration is both personal and powerful: "O Lord, You are my God." It's not distant or formal—it's intimate and rooted in a relationship. He speaks from a heart that knows God's character and has witnessed His faithfulness over time.

Even when life felt uncertain, Isaiah praised God for His "wonderful things"—not just the visible blessings, but the unseen ways God was working all along. His plans, formed long ago, always come to pass in perfect faithfulness and truth.

This verse reminds us that God's promises are never broken. What He began in your life, He will complete. Every delay, every trial, and every victory is woven into His faithful design. When you don't understand His ways, you can still trust Him.

Lord, You are my God, and I exalt Your name. Thank You for Your faithfulness that never fails and Your truth that stands forever. Even when I cannot see the whole picture, I trust Your plans for my life. Teach me to praise You in all seasons, knowing You are good and Your works are wonderful.

In Jesus' name I pray, Amen.

Scripture Reflection

Day 3

*"Your unfailing love is better than life itself;
How I praise you! I will praise you as long as I
live, lifting up my hands to you in prayer."*

Psalm 63:3-4

Praising My Way to My Breakthrough

There is no love like the love of God. His love reaches deeper than our pain, stretches wider than our mistakes, and rises higher than our understanding. David understood this truth in the wilderness — even without comfort, crown, or company, he found everything he needed in God's presence.

When we say, "Your love is better than life," we are declaring that nothing this world offers can compare to the joy, peace, and security found in Him. Life itself is temporary, but His love is eternal. It restores the brokenhearted, lifts the weary, and fills the empty places of the soul.

Let your praise today come from that place of deep gratitude — not for what He's done, but for who He is. His love never fails, never fades, and never leaves.

Father, thank you for another chance to get it right in your sight. I know that I have not been obedient and rebelled, but here I am, Father, willing to answer the call you planned for my life.

In Your Son Jesus' name, I pray, Amen.

Praising My Way to My Breakthrough

Scripture Reflection

Day 4

"The Lord is my strength and shield. I trust Him with all my heart. He helps me, and my heart is filled with joy. I burst out in songs of thanksgiving."

Psalm 28:7

Praising My Way to My Breakthrough

Praise to God is our way of expressing our gratitude and faithfulness toward Him. When praising God, we show Him admiration for all He has done in our lives. Praise is something that we do to usher in the Spirit of the living God, to be in His presence. Praise tears down walls, breaks chains, and sets the captives free. Praise is honoring God for loving us through His Son, Jesus, by shedding His blood so that we can live in liberation from the bondage of sin. Praise is lifted hands, open hearts to receive, tears flowing, and words of Thanksgiving from our hearts are uttered to Him out of our mouths. Your breakthrough is in your praise.

Most heavenly and gracious Father, thank you for another opportunity to give thanksgiving to your name, the name above all names. You are to be glorified and exalted. I love you, Lord, and I will forever call You my Lord and Savior.

In Jesus' name, Amen.

Praising My Way to My Breakthrough

Scripture Reflection

Day 5:

"Let all that I am praise the Lord; with my whole heart, I will praise His holy name."

Psalm 103:1

True praise begins in the depths of our being — every thought, every emotion, every breath offered in worship. When we say, "Let all that I am praise the Lord with my whole heart," we are committing ourselves fully to God, not just in words, but in spirit, mind, and actions.

Wholehearted praise recognizes God's mercy, love, and faithfulness. It turns gratitude into worship and worship into a lifestyle. Every part of you — your soul, mind, body, and spirit — becomes an instrument for glorifying Him.

Let today be a day of total surrender in praise. Offer Him your thoughts, your time, your talents, and your trust. When every part of you lifts His name, His presence fills you with joy, peace, and strength.

Gracious heavenly Father, I want to start with a thank you! You were so faithful and patient with me when you didn't have to be. I will forever be grateful for the love you have bestowed upon me. I give you all the glory and honor that is due to you with gladness. I love you and couldn't see life without you.

In your Son Jesus' name, I pray, Amen.

Praising My Way to My Breakthrough

Scripture Reflection

Praising My Way to My Breakthrough

Day 6

"Around midnight Paul and Silas were praying and singing hymns to God, and the other prisoners were listening."

Acts 16:25

Praising My Way to My Breakthrough

At midnight — the darkest hour — Paul and Silas chose to praise instead of complain. Bound by chains and surrounded by despair, they lifted their voices in worship. Their praise became a key that unlocked not only their freedom but the hearts of those who heard them.

Midnight moments come to all of us — seasons of uncertainty, pain, or waiting. Yet, it's in those moments that our praise carries the greatest power. When we worship through the tears, God moves through the walls that hold us captive.

Your midnight may look different, but the same God who heard Paul and Silas hears you now. Praise turns prisons into pulpits, chains into testimonies, and sorrow into songs of deliverance.
So when the night feels long and heavy, lift your voice — for dawn is on the way, and breakthrough is already being released in the atmosphere.

Holy Father, magnificent one of Glory! You are the chain-breaker and curse-breaker. You are the giver of life and blessings. You are a strong tower in times of trouble. I thank you for being there for me when no one else was there to lean on and to rescue me. You are my refuge and strength.

In Your Son Jesus' name, I pray, Amen.

Scripture Reflection

Praising My Way to My Breakthrough

Day 7

"I will praise you, Lord, with all my heart; I will tell of all the marvelous things you have done."

Psalm 9:1

Praising My Way to My Breakthrough

True praise flows from the heart — not just from the lips. It's born from remembrance, gratitude, and love for the One who has carried us through every season. When David declared, "I will praise You, Lord, with all my heart," he was offering more than a song — he was offering himself.

To praise God with all your heart means to hold nothing back. It's praising Him in joy and in sorrow, in certainty and in waiting. It's the kind of worship that invites His presence to dwell and His glory to shine through your life.

Each time you reflect on His goodness — every prayer answered, every storm calmed, every moment of peace — let your heart overflow in praise. For our God is faithful, and He deserves our whole heart, not just a portion of it.

Most precious heavenly Father, I vow to praise you. You are an amazing God! I can express my gratitude for your blessings and love you have shown me over the years. You are the epitome of the true meaning of love, and there is no greater love I know. I honor you and give you all the glory.

In Jesus' name, I pray, Amen.

Scripture Reflection

Praising My Way to My Breakthrough

Day 8

"Great is the Lord! He is most worthy of praise! No one can measure his greatness."

Psalm 145:3

There is none like our God. His greatness cannot be measured, and His power cannot be contained. From the rising of the sun to its setting, His name is worthy to be praised. When we reflect on His goodness — His mercy that endures, His grace that sustains, His love that never fails — our hearts cannot help but rejoice.

To declare that "Great is the Lord" is more than an expression of admiration; it's an act of faith. It is a reminder that even when we don't understand His ways, we can trust His heart. Every breath we breathe and every blessing we see is a reflection of His greatness.

Let your praise rise higher today. Lift your voice, your heart, and your hands in awe of the One who reigns above all. For our God is not only great — He is good, gracious, and faithful in all His ways.

Dear heavenly my Lord and Savior Jesus Christ. There is none like you who can touch my heart like you do. You are the good, good Father and worthy to be praised. I love you and adore you. As I live each day, I must give you all the glory.

In Jesus' name, I pray, Amen.

Praising My Way to My Breakthrough

Scripture Reflection

Praising My Way to My Breakthrough

Day 9

"Why am I discouraged? Why is my heart so sad? I will put my hope in God! I will praise him again- my Savior and my God!"

Psalm 42:11 NLT

Praising My Way to My Breakthrough

There are moments when the weight of life feels unbearable—when discouragement creeps in and your spirit feels low. The psalmist knew this feeling well, yet instead of surrendering to despair, he spoke directly to his soul. He reminded himself of the truth: Hope in God… I shall yet praise Him.

Praise has the power to lift us out of discouragement. Even when your emotions are heavy, praise redirects your focus from the problem to the Promise Keeper. It strengthens your faith and stirs your spirit to remember that God is still present, still faithful, and still working on your behalf.

When you declare praise in dark seasons, you're telling your soul that despair will not win. Hope will rise, and joy will return, because God is your help and the source of your strength.

Father, when my heart feels heavy, remind me to hope in You. Lift my spirit through the power of praise. Help me to remember that You are the light in my darkness and the strength of my life. I will yet praise You, for You are my God.

In Jesus' name I pray, Amen.

Scripture Reflection

Praising My Way to My Breakthrough

Day 10

"For you formed my inward parts; you knitted me together in my mother's womb. I praise you, for I am fearfully and wonderfully made. Wonderful are your works; my soul knows it very well."

Psalm 139:13:14

God made us in His image. He is to be feared, so He made us fearful. He is a wonder, so we are wonderfully made. God designed us to glorify Him. It is in His plan for everyone to fulfill a purpose we are predestined for. We are a miracle, a sign, and a wonder. It does not matter what race, gender, or physical state each of us is born into. God made us to serve a purpose, and that is to do His will His way. We are to praise, reverence, and worship Him in spirit and truth. Jesus paid the ultimate price to end sin, so it is our duty as believers to kill flesh, carry our cross, and win souls through the gospel of Jesus, our Lord and Savior. We are different on the outside, but we all carry the same DNA of our Father in Heaven.

Heavenly Father, I thank you and give all praises unto you. I ask you, Father, to give me a heart of flesh to be in repentance and give me the spiritual eyes to see others as you see them. I want to see others beyond their flaws, just like you see me beyond my flaws. I surrendered my heart to you and asked you to give me the strength to love as you do.

In Jesus Christ's name I pray, Amen.

Scripture Reflection

Praising My Way to My Breakthrough

Day 11

"I will always bless the Lord; his praise shall continually be in my mouth. My soul makes its boast in the Lord; let the humble hear and be glad ."

Psalm 34:1-2

Praising My Way to My Breakthrough

Praise is not meant for moments of comfort only — it is the melody of a heart that trusts God in every season. David spoke these words not from a throne, but from a place of hiding and uncertainty. Yet even there, he made a choice: to bless the Lord at all times.

To continually praise God is to declare that His goodness is not dependent on our circumstances. It is an act of faith, a spiritual weapon, and a statement of love. Every time you choose praise over worry, gratitude over complaint, and worship over fear, you open the door for God's presence to fill your situation.

Let His praise be your constant song — morning and night, in joy and in trial. For when praise becomes your posture, peace becomes your portion.

Father, I thank you and glorify your name. Thank you for your forgiveness and love. You have been so patient with me, and I thank you for your long-suffering. Everything I am and who I am, I owe it all to you and only you. Thank you for no longer remembering my sins and for giving me the ability to forget others' sins. All praises and honor are due to you, and I am glad to praise your name.

In Jesus Christ's name I pray, Amen.

Scripture Reflection

Praising My Way to My Breakthrough

Day 12

"My mouth is filled with your praise,

and with your glory all day."

Psalm 71:8

To glorify God is to sing praises to Him out of our mouths to usher in His presence. For Him to fill the atmosphere with His supernatural anointing and to drench us with His oil and blow in the fresh wind of His Spirit. Praise is a chance to be intimate with our Father in a worship experience from His throne room. Praise is our way of showing gratitude and adoration to our Father. Praise to me is picturing myself standing in the middle of a mellow field with my face looking to the sky, eyes closed, and tears begin to flow because of the joy He gives. My arms stretched open with mild wind blowing, no noise, only hearing the voice of God and basking in His presence. Soaking in His peace and resting on His promises.

Father, thank you for hands to clap, feet to stomp, ears to hear, and eyes to see your Goodness and glory. Thank you for a mouth to sing your praises and a willingness to serve you. Cleanse me and drench me with your oil so that I may remain in truth. You are all I need to get through the days, whether it's good or bad. I honor you and give you all the praise.

In Jesus' name I pray, Amen.

Scripture Reflection

Day 13

"And I heard every creature in heaven and on earth and under the earth and in the sea, and all that is in them, saying, "To him who sits on the throne and to the Lamb be blessing and honor and glory and might forever and ever!"

Revelation 5:13

This verse paints a breathtaking picture of universal worship. Every voice in heaven, on earth, and beneath the earth joins together in one mighty chorus, proclaiming the greatness of God and the glory of the Lamb, Jesus Christ. Nothing and no one is silent—every part of creation lifts up praise to the One who reigns forever.

This moment reminds us that praise is eternal. It's not just something we do here on earth; it's the language of heaven. When we praise God now, we are joining the heavenly symphony that never ceases to glorify Him.

Even in times of hardship or uncertainty, remember: you are part of a greater song. Your voice matters in the eternal worship of the King. Every word of praise you speak echoes in eternity and aligns your heart with the everlasting kingdom of God.

Lord, You are worthy of all blessing, honor, glory, and power. I join with all creation to praise Your holy name. Thank You for redeeming me through the Lamb, Jesus Christ. Let my life be a continual song of worship that glorifies You forever and ever.

In Jesus' name I pray, Amen.

Scripture Reflection

Praising My Way to My Breakthrough

Day 14

"Let the word of Christ dwell in you richly, teaching and admonishing one another in all wisdom, singing psalms and hymns and spiritual songs, with thankfulness in your hearts to God."

Colossians 3:16

The Word of Christ is living, powerful, and filled with grace. When we allow His Word to dwell richly within us, it becomes the source of our peace, our wisdom, and our praise. It shapes our thoughts, guides our decisions, and fills our hearts with songs of joy.

To "dwell richly" means more than simply reading Scripture — it means allowing God's truth to take root deep within our spirit. When His Word lives in us, it changes the way we speak, think, and love. Praise flows naturally from a heart that is nourished by the Word of God.

Let the Word fill your home, your mind, and your conversations. Let it overflow in worship and encouragement to others. For when the Word dwells richly, Christ is glorified richly through you.

Heavenly Father, you know I will have good days and bad days. No matter what my day holds, I will always give you praise and honor.

In Jesus' name, I pray, Amen.

Scripture Reflection

Day 15

*"Oh, give thanks to the Lord; call upon his name;
Make known his deeds among the people!"*

Psalm 105:1

Gratitude is the language of a heart that knows God's faithfulness. When we give thanks to the Lord, we are not only acknowledging His goodness — we are proclaiming His power and presence in our lives. Every blessing, seen and unseen, is a reminder that God's hand is upon us.

To call upon His name is to draw near to Him in trust and devotion. It's an act of worship that opens the heavens and invites His peace to dwell within us. As we remember His mighty deeds — His healing, His protection, His provision — our praise becomes a testimony that draws others closer to Him.

Let your gratitude be heard. Speak of His goodness, sing of His mercy, and share His love. A thankful heart is a vessel through which God's glory is revealed.

Father, God, give me the strength and the boldness to tell the world who you are and all that you have done in my life.

In Jesus' name I pray, Amen.

Scripture Reflection

Day 16

*"I will extol you, my God and King,
and bless your name forever and ever."*

Psalm 145:1

To extol God is to lift Him high — to honor His majesty and proclaim His greatness over our lives. David recognized God not only as a personal Savior but also as the sovereign King over all creation. Extolling Him acknowledges His power, His wisdom, and His unchanging faithfulness.

Worship that exalts God strengthens our faith. When we lift His name above every challenge, every fear, and every circumstance, we are declaring that He alone is worthy of all glory. Our words, thoughts, and actions become a reflection of His sovereignty.

Let today be a day of exaltation. Speak His praises boldly. Let your heart and lips honor the King who reigns forever, for He is good, and His mercy endures throughout all generations.

Father in Heaven, I ask that you give me the tenacity to endure to the end to praise you. I bless your name forever and forever.

In Jesus' name I pray, Amen.

Praising My Way to My Breakthrough

Scripture Reflection

Praising My Way to My Breakthrough

Day 17

"For it is written, 'As I live, says the Lord, every knee shall bow to me, and every tongue shall confess to God."

Roman 14:11

Praising My Way to My Breakthrough

This verse is a powerful reminder of the absolute sovereignty of God. One day, every person—great and small, believer and unbeliever will acknowledge the Lord's glory. Every knee will bow, and every tongue will confess that He alone is worthy of praise.

But as believers, we don't have to wait for that day. We can bow our hearts now in humility, gratitude, and reverence. We can use our voices today to confess His goodness, to praise His name, and to honor His authority over our lives.

Praise is our willing surrender—it's the act of saying, "Lord, You reign over me." When we bow before Him now, we are not only aligning ourselves with His will, but also walking in the peace, strength, and joy that come from recognizing His power and presence.

Lord, You alone are worthy of all praise and honor. I bow before You in reverence and love. Help me to confess Your greatness not only with my lips but with my life. Let everything I do bring You glory, and may my praise be a reflection of Your eternal reign.

In Jesus' name I pray, Amen.

Scripture Reflection

Day 18

"Heal me, O Lord, and I shall be healed; save me, and I shall be saved, for you are my praise."

Jeremiah 17:14

Healing begins with a cry to God — a declaration that we trust His power over our bodies, minds, and spirits. When we say, "Heal me, O Lord, and I shall be healed," we are exercising faith, surrendering our pain, and inviting God's restorative touch into every part of our lives.

This verse reminds us that God is the ultimate source of healing. He not only restores what is broken but also strengthens what is weak. Our response of praise — even in the midst of need — aligns our hearts with His power and mercy, opening the door for miracles and transformation.

Let your heart speak to God today. Bring your burdens, your aches, and your worries, and declare that His healing power will flow through you. Trust that He is working all things together for your restoration.

Father, thank you for your healing power. I thank you for sharing your knowledge and understanding with me.

In Jesus' name I pray, Amen.

Praising My Way to My Breakthrough

Scripture Reflection

Day 19

"Finally, brothers, whatever is true, whatever is honorable, whatever is just, whatever is pure, whatever is lovely, whatever is commendable, if there is any excellence, if there is anything worthy of praise, think about these things."

Philippians 4:8

Praising My Way to My Breakthrough

Our thoughts are the seeds that shape our days. What we allow to take root in our minds will eventually grow into the words we speak and the actions we take. Paul reminds us in Philippians 4:8 that the mind of a believer should be centered on things that reflect God's nature—truth, purity, love, and virtue. When we choose to praise instead of complain, to meditate on God's goodness instead of life's disappointments, we begin to transform our atmosphere. Praise renews the mind. It lifts our hearts out of anxiety and ushers in divine peace. God wants us to live in a space where our thoughts glorify Him, even in our trials. As we think on things that are of good report, we are reminded of who God is and what He has already done. Our thoughts become a sanctuary of worship, and from that place, breakthroughs are born.

Father God, you are worthy of praise and glory. Thank you for breathing your spirit into me and giving me another day to be in your presence.

In Jesus' name I pray, Amen.

Scripture Reflection

Day 20

"And you will say in that day: 'Give thanks to the Lord, call upon his name, make known his deeds among the people, proclaim that his name is exalted."

Isaiah 12:4

God's people are called to respond to His goodness with thanksgiving. Gratitude is not just a polite gesture; it is an acknowledgment of His power, His mercy, and His faithfulness. When we give thanks, we declare that our hope and joy are rooted in Him alone.

This verse reminds us that even in the midst of change, uncertainty, or victory, our hearts should overflow with praise. Sharing God's deeds among others magnifies His glory and strengthens the faith of those around us. Every act of gratitude becomes a testimony that draws others closer to the Lord. Let today be a day of intentional thanksgiving. Speak His name aloud, remember His works, and let your praise inspire all who hear it.

Heavenly Father, you are my salvation, strength, and peace. Your words are the lyrics to my song of praise. Thank you for all that you are in my life and my family's life. Calling on your name is the only way to overcome the fears and anxiety of everyday life. I thank You for not turning Your wrath on me when I went against Your will. I thank You for past grace and mercy, and I am asking You, Father, to expand more of Your grace and mercy over my life because I will make mistakes. Thank you for loving me and showing me that I am important and valuable and that I am the apple of your eye. I thank you for your Son Jesus for giving His life so I can have mine here. Father, you will forever be the head of my life, and I will always love you and glorify your name. You are worthy to be praised, and I will forever exalt Your name. Father God, thank you for coming into my life and blessing me the way you do. Thank you for believing in me when others counted me out.

In Jesus' name I pray, Amen.

Praising My Way to My Breakthrough

Scripture Reflection

Praising My Way to My Breakthrough

Day 21

"I will give thanks to you, O Lord, among the peoples; I will sing praises to you among the nations."

Psalm 108:3

David's heart overflowed with praise that could not be contained. His worship wasn't private—it was public, bold, and contagious. He declared, "I will praise You among the peoples." His desire was that the whole world would know the goodness, mercy, and faithfulness of God.

This verse reminds us that praise is not meant to be hidden. When we speak of God's goodness openly, we bear witness to His power and inspire others to seek Him. Our testimonies become songs that echo beyond our own lives.

In a world filled with noise, negativity, and distraction, your praise is a light that draws others toward hope. Every time you lift your voice—whether in song, prayer, or gratitude—you are declaring to the world that God is worthy.

Lord, I will praise You among the nations! Let my voice bring You glory and let my life be a song of thanksgiving. May my worship reach beyond walls and touch hearts that need Your presence. Give me boldness to declare Your name in every place I go.

In Jesus' name I pray, Amen.

Praising My Way to My Breakthrough

Scripture Reflection

Day 22

"Blessed be the God and Father of our Lord Jesus Christ, who has blessed us in Christ with every spiritual blessing in the heavenly places."

Ephesians 1:3

In Christ, we are not waiting to be blessed — we are already blessed. These blessings are not bound by time, circumstance, or earthly possessions. They are spiritual gifts — peace that passes understanding, joy that cannot be shaken, strength to endure, and love that overflows.

The "heavenly places" remind us that our true identity and inheritance are rooted above, not below. When we walk in Christ, we carry the atmosphere of heaven into every situation on earth. Even when life feels uncertain, we are seated with Him in victory. So today, lift your heart in gratitude. You are not chasing blessings — you are walking in them. Christ Himself is your portion, your covering, and your abundance.

Thank you, Heavenly Father, for Your love, mercy, and glorious grace that You have extended through Your Son Jesus. Because of Your Son Jesus, I am redeemed and made whole. Thank you for giving me access to your wisdom and knowledge, and forgiving all my sins because of your Son, Jesus. I said it many times before, and I will most likely repeat it. I will praise and worship You in my going out and my coming in. Daily, search my heart so that I am in preparation for Your return. I asked that you continue to convict me and show me those hidden things in my heart so I will not sin against you. I give you all the praises, honor, and glory to my Savior and Lord, Jesus.

Scripture Reflection

Day 23

"From the same mouth come blessing and cursing. My brothers, these things ought not to be so."

James 3:10

Our words hold incredible power—they can heal or hurt, bless or curse, build up or tear down. James reminds us that it is inconsistent for a heart that loves God to speak both blessings and curses. If our hearts are filled with His Spirit, then our mouths should reflect His grace.

Every word we speak reveals the condition of our hearts. When we speak life, hope, and encouragement, we reflect the nature of Christ within us. But when we speak negatively, we hinder the flow of God's peace and blessings in our lives and the lives of others.

This verse calls us to a higher standard—to let our mouths become instruments of praise. When we choose to bless instead of curse, to encourage instead of criticize, we honor God and release His power through our words.

Lord, help me to use my words for Your glory. Let my mouth overflow with praise, not negativity. Purify my heart so that everything I say reflects Your love and truth. May my words be a source of life, encouragement, and peace to those around me.

In Jesus' name I pray, Amen.

Praising My Way to My Breakthrough

Scripture Reflection

Day 24

Praising My Way to My Breakthrough

"Then Job arose and tore his robe and shaved his head and fell on the ground and worshiped. And he said, "Naked I came from my mother's womb, and naked shall I return. The Lord gave, and the Lord has taken away; blessed be the name of the Lord." In all this, Job did not sin or charge God with wrong."

Job 1:20-22

Praising My Way to My Breakthrough

Job's response to unimaginable loss reveals the depth of true faith. He grieved deeply—tore his robe, shaved his head—but even in his sorrow, he worshiped. Job didn't deny his pain, but he refused to let it silence his praise. His heart declared, "Blessed be the name of the Lord," even when everything around him was falling apart.

This passage teaches us that worship isn't reserved for the mountaintop; it's often birthed in the valley. Real praise is not dependent on how we feel—it's rooted in who God is. Even when life takes away what we hold dear, God remains good, faithful, and worthy of our praise.

When you choose to worship through your tears, heaven takes notice. Your praise in the storm becomes a testimony that speaks louder.

Father, in moments of loss and disappointment, help me to keep my eyes on You. Teach me to worship through the pain, to bless Your name even when I don't understand. Strengthen my faith like Job's, so that my praise remains steadfast no matter what comes my way.

In Jesus' name I pray, Amen.

Praising My Way to My Breakthrough

Scripture Reflection

Praising My Way to My Breakthrough

Day 25

"And day by day, attending the temple together and breaking bread in their homes, they received their food with glad and generous hearts, praising God and having favor with all the people. And the Lord added to their number day by day those who were being saved ."

Acts 2:46-47

Praising My Way to My Breakthrough

The early church lived in a rhythm of praise, unity, and gratitude. Their devotion wasn't occasional—it was daily. They gathered in the temple to worship, shared meals together, and celebrated the goodness of God with joyful and sincere hearts.

Because their praise flowed from genuine love and unity, God's presence was among them. Their consistency in worship and fellowship became a witness to others, drawing souls into the kingdom. Praise and community worked hand in hand—worship strengthened their faith, and fellowship strengthened their hearts.

This passage reminds us that praise is powerful when it's consistent and shared. When believers come together in one accord, with hearts full of gratitude, heaven responds. Our daily acts of worship—prayer, gratitude, kindness, and fellowship—open doors for God's blessings to multiply in our lives and in the lives of others.

Lord, thank You for the gift of fellowship and the power of praise. Help me to worship You daily with a glad and generous heart. Unite me with others in love, and let my life reflect Your joy and peace. May my praise draw others closer to You.

In Jesus' name I pray, Amen.

Scripture Reflection

Day 26

*"In God, whose word I praise, in God I trust;
I shall not be afraid. What can flesh do to me?"*

Psalm 56:4

Praising My Way to My Breakthrough

To praise God through His Word is to acknowledge that His promises are true and unchanging. Every verse, every instruction, and every declaration in Scripture points to His faithfulness and love. When we trust in Him, we are placing our confidence not in the shifting circumstances of life, but in the eternal truth of His Word.

Trust and praise are inseparable. When we believe God's Word, our hearts respond in worship, gratitude, and obedience. Even in the midst of trials, His Word is a firm foundation that gives courage, hope, and peace. Let today be a day of alignment with God's truth. Speak His promises, meditate on His Word, and trust Him fully. Your praise becomes a living testimony of faith in action.

Loving and faithful Father in Heaven, here I am on this day and every day giving Thanks, honor, and glory to Your name. I thank you for vindicating me and my family from every curse spoken word, exposing the enemy of its plots and plans, and rerouting every demonic arrow he had set up to destroy. Thank you for giving me the boldness to stand up for what is right and speak against what is wrong. I trust You and only You to the fullest because You have never changed against me, and I don't believe You ever will. You are holy and righteous. You are my refuge and fortress in times of trouble. My comfort and peace in times of chaos.

Praising My Way to My Breakthrough

Lord, You are welcome into my life daily without my permission because I cannot get through any day without You, and I will not try to. I ask that You be the light to my path. I need Your wisdom, knowledge, and understanding.

In Jesus' name, Amen.

Praising My Way to My Breakthrough

Scripture Reflection

Praising My Way to My Breakthrough

Day 27

"To you, O God of my fathers, I give thanks and praise, for you have given me wisdom and might, and have now made known to me what we asked of you, for you have made known to us the king's matter."

Daniel 2:23

Giving thanks is powerful, but adding praise elevates our hearts even higher. When we say, "To You, O God of my father, I give thanks and praise," we are acknowledging God's enduring faithfulness across generations. He is the same yesterday, today, and forever — a God of wisdom, power, and love.

Praise is more than words; it is a declaration of trust, a recognition of His majesty, and a reflection of our gratitude. As we honor Him for all that He has done, we align ourselves with His purposes and invite His presence into our lives.

Let your heart today overflow in both thanks and praise. Celebrate His goodness, remember His faithfulness, and declare His glory over your life and family.

Praise the Lord for a new day. You deserve to be honored and glorified for all that you do—and continue to do—in my life and for my family. I thank You, Father, for making known to me what is ahead, whether it be in a vision, dream, or prophecy. Father, without Your wisdom, knowledge, and understanding, I would be lost in my way of thinking. That is why I need to seek Your kingdom daily and throughout the day. I must search Your heart, and You search mine, because I do not want to go through the rest of my life lacking and broken. This is the only way I know how to get through my day: by consistently being in Your presence. I love You, Father, and Your Son, Jesus, and because of Your beloved Son, I get to see another day to witness Your glory.

In Jesus' name, Amen.

Praising My Way to My Breakthrough

Scripture Reflection

Day 28

"But the hour is coming, and is now here when the true worshipers will worship the Father in spirit and truth, for the Father is seeking such people to worship him."

John 4:23

Praising My Way to My Breakthrough

Jesus reminds us that authentic worship transcends rituals, buildings, and schedules. The "hour" He speaks of is a moment — and a movement — where hearts fully surrender to God in spirit and truth. Worship becomes not just an action, but a lifestyle. When we worship in spirit and truth, we align ourselves with God's presence, experiencing His peace, joy, and guidance. It is in these moments that heaven touches earth, and our praise becomes a living testimony of God's glory.

Let this truth inspire you today: God is seeking worshipers who will offer Him their genuine hearts. The hour is now. Don't wait to lift your voice, to give thanks, and to honor Him in every part of your life.

Heavenly Father, thank You for another day of life. Another day to bless You with my highest praise and adoration to show You how grateful I am to be in Your presence. My praise and worship are to engage Your spirit and pursue You in truth so that I am transformed by the renewing of my mind to be like Yours. I need more of Your wisdom, knowledge, and understanding. No other god can compare to You, nor love like You. You are the true and living God, and Jesus is the true Messiah and King. I surrender my life to you and only you.

In Jesus' name I pray, Amen.

Praising My Way to My Breakthrough

Scripture Reflection

Day 29

"For all the gods of the people are worthless idols, but the Lord made the heavens. Splendor and majesty are before Him, strength and joy are in his place."

1 Chronicles 16:26-27

The world may offer many distractions, false promises, and counterfeit sources of hope. Yet the psalmist reminds us that all other "gods" are powerless — empty and fleeting. True power, creation, and life come from the Lord alone.

When we worship the true God, we release our hearts from the chains of deception and idolatry. Our faith is anchored in the One who made the heavens, the earth, and all that is within them. Every time we lift our hearts in praise, we are declaring the futility of idols and the sufficiency of God.

Let your focus today remain on the Lord, the only true God. He alone is worthy of your worship, your devotion, and your trust. Every act of obedience and praise affirms His glory above all else.

Most gracious and heavenly Father, thank You for another day's journey. Thank You for life, health, and strength, and most importantly, thank You for grace and mercy. Because of Your Son Jesus, grace and mercy will follow me, knowing that I am unworthy of it. Let the blast of breath from Your nostrils rebuke the enemy from restraining me from getting to my purpose and destiny. Let the enemy see Your arm in this battle because the battle is Yours. I look to You, Father, for direction and the Holy Spirit to orient me daily to walk in the fullness of Your perfect will. I will always be in praise

Praising My Way to My Breakthrough

mode because I know that is where my breakthrough dwells. You are God over Heaven and earth. There is no track record of the other gods, and there will never be.

In Jesus' mighty name, Amen.

Praising My Way to My Breakthrough

Scripture Reflection

Day 30

"Filled with the fruit of righteousness that comes through Jesus Christ, to the glory and praise of God."

Philippians 1:11

Paul reminds us that a life rooted in Christ will naturally bear the fruit of righteousness. Just as a healthy tree produces good fruit, a heart filled with the Spirit produces praise, goodness, and godly character.

This fruit isn't something we create by our own strength—it grows as we remain connected to Jesus, the true vine. When we walk with Him daily, His love shapes our attitudes, His peace fills our hearts, and His righteousness shines through our actions. The result? Our lives become living testimonies that bring glory and praise to God.

True praise is more than words or songs—it's a lifestyle. It's reflected in how we treat others, how we respond to challenges, and how we live out our faith. When our hearts are filled with Christ, our lives become a continual offering of praise to the One who makes us whole.

Lord, fill me with the fruit of righteousness that comes through Jesus Christ. Let everything I do and say bring glory to Your name. Help me to live a life that reflects Your goodness and love, so that my praise is not just spoken—but seen.

Praising My Way to My Breakthrough

Scripture Reflection

About the Author

Debbie Snooks-Aiken is a woman of faith with a heart devoted to uplifting others through the power of praise and worship. She believes that praise is not just an expression but a powerful weapon that breaks chains, ushers in healing, and draws us closer to Jesus Christ.

In her inspiring book, 30 Days of Praise, Debbie reminds readers that our praise is an act of gratitude for God's grace, mercy, and blessings. It is a love language to our Savior and a key to unlocking spiritual breakthrough.

Debbie's passion is to encourage believers to develop a deeper relationship with God through daily praise and thanksgiving. She desires to see lives transformed as people discover the freedom and joy that come from true worship.

When she's not writing, Debbie enjoys spending time with her family, serving in ministry, and inspiring others to walk boldly in their faith.

30 Days of Praise is a heartfelt invitation to praise your way into purpose, peace, and power.

Made in the USA
Monee, IL
03 May 2026